Gotti:

John Gotti American Mafia Boss

Daniel Brand

including specific information will be considered an illegal act irrespective of if it is done electronically or in print. This extends to creating a secondary or tertiary copy of the work or a recorded copy and is only allowed with express written consent from the Publisher. All additional right reserved.

The information in the following pages is broadly considered to be a truthful and accurate account of facts and as such any inattention, use or misuse of the information in question by the reader will render any resulting actions solely under their purview. There are no scenarios in which the publisher or the original author of this work can be in any fashion deemed liable for any hardship or damages that may befall them after undertaking information described herein.

Additionally, the information in the following pages is intended only for informational purposes and should thus be thought of as universal. As befitting its nature, it is presented without assurance regarding its prolonged validity or interim quality. Trademarks that are mentioned are done without written consent and can in no way be considered an endorsement from the trademark holder.

TABLE OF CONTENTS

Introduction

J ohn Gotti was a New York City gangster who went on to become the head of the most powerful crime family in the city, the Gambinos. Gotti's meteoric rise and fall was said to have radically, and irreparably change the American Mafia forever. When he rose to power in 1986 the Gambino family was bringing in hundreds of millions of dollars every year through a variety of illegal activities including gambling, numbers, pornography, extortion, prostitution, racketeering, bookmaking, drug trafficking, kickbacks from labor unions, loan sharking, hijacking, waste management, construction and other assorted criminal activities.

At the peak of his empire, Gotti was known around the world as the Dapper Don due to his flamboyant style and outspoken personality. His penchant for being in front of the camera marked a distinct change from others who had previously held his position and earned him a place in the hearts of the general public as well. This wasn't his only nickname, however as a number of high-profile trials in the 1980s saw him acquitted time and again. This was arranged due to an elaborate web of intimidation, bribery and jury tampering, but the public ate it up regardless.

Gotti is eventually brought down when another member of the family Salvatore Gravano provided states evidence on Gotti after the FBI arranged for him to hear some disparaging remarks Gotti made about him. In 1992 he was convicted of loansharking, tax evasion, extortion, illegal gambling, obstruction of justice, racketeering, conspiracy to commit murder and multiple homicides for which he ultimately received life in prison. He died of throat cancer in 2002.

What makes Gotti such an interesting case to study, however, is what his time in charge did for organized crime in New York as a whole. While his rule may have ended in the 90s, his influence is still being felt by the made men of New York City today. The story you will find in the following pages shows how Gotti orchestrated a change in the way the American Mafia operated from a tight-lipped secret society to a household name. This, in turn, made it much easier for informants of all sorts to work their way into the system, destroying much of its power in the process.

While for the more than 50 years the very existence of the American Mafia was in doubt, by the time Gotti died, more than half of all of the soldiers in the family were estimated to be in prison and another third where expected or known to be informing for one agency or other. Gotti certainly left a legacy for the Family, though likely not the one he would have preferred.

Chapter 1
GETTING IN

G otti was born in the Bronx on Oct 27, 1940 to Pilomena and John Joseph Gotti and while both of his parents were born in America, all four of his grandparents came from San Giuseppe Vesuviano in Naples. He was the fifth out of 13 children and one of five Gottis to ultimately join the Gambino crime family. His brother Gene Gotti joined before him, Peter Gotti was brought in after his rise to power in 1988 and Richard and Vincent Gotti were both initiated prior to his death in 2002.

The Gotti's grew up in poverty with John Joseph working as a day laborer and spending most of his meager pay in illegal gambling parlors. This inability to provide for his family is something that the younger John took to heart and never stopped resenting about his father. This desire to make something of himself didn't extend to his school work, however, and Gotti had an early history of truancy as well as violence and of bullying other students. He stopped attending high school at the age of 16.

Prior to joining the Gambinos, Gotti was involved with numerous street gangs that were indirectly associated with the mafia as early as the age of 12. At the age of 14 these associations led him to attempt to steal a large cement mixer from a construction site near his home. The heist went sideways and he dropped the mixer, crushing his toes and leaving him with a pronounced limp that stayed with him the rest of his life.

At the age of 16, after leaving school behind, Gotti committed himself to the Fulton-Rockaway Boys gang full time. There he would meet future friends and fellow Gambinos

Wilfred "Willie Boy" Johnson and Angelo Ruggiero. Two years later he would meet his future wife, Victoria DiGiorgio, and they were married in March of 1962. They would ultimately go on to have five children, Victoria, John Jr., Angel and Peter before 1980 and Gotti would attempt to go straight for a while when Victoria was born. Not being a part of the life didn't suit him however and before 1968 ended he had already been back to jail twice.

Stepping up his game

As a member of the boy's gang, Gotti spent time frequently running errands for Carmine Fatico who was a capo with the Anastasia crime family that ultimately became the Gambino crime family after the murder of Albert Anastasia. Gotti also regularly carried out truck hijackings at the future John F. Kennedy International Airport along with brother Gene and fellow gang member Ruggiero. It was on one of these jobs that Gotti first came into contact with

Joseph Massino, the eventual head of the Bonanno family. Much of Gotti's young life would be full of such meetings, and Gotti made sure to take full advantage of these types of connections as often as possible as an adult. What's more, he also formed a distinct distaste for those who had not spent time among the rank and file, building up these connections from scratch as opposed to whose family knows whom.

It was also around this time that Gotti first met his future friend and mentor Aniello "Niel" Dellacroce an underboss for the future Gambino family. Dellacroce had spent most of his life working for Anastasia and regularly told Gotti stories of the glory days of the Family under his rule, though if he had known what the young man was going to do with the inspiration he likely wouldn't have bothered. Gotti would later go on to take Anastasi as his role model for his future organized crime career. Each family was organized in the same fashion, each family boss would be assisted by an underboss who would directly command the captains, or capos, who in turn would each control their own unit of soldiers. Each family was also consulted by a type of family lawyer and advisor known as a consigliere. Each member of the family management team would receive a share of what the people underneath them brought in and pay a tithe to those above them. This system was originally designed to ensure that those at the top were very difficult to pin actual crimes on, and it worked very well until John Gotti came along.

In February 1968 employees with United Airlines fingered Gotti as the person who had signed for stolen merchandise from their terminal. The FBI arrested him soon after and then arrested him for the same crime again a few months later after he had been released on bail. The second time he was attempting to steal $50,000 worth of cigarettes while on the New Jersey Turnpike. Before the end of 1968, Gotti was also arrested for stealing cargo from Northwest Airlines and was finally sentenced to three years in prison after the cigarette theft was dropped.

Ruggiero went with Gotti to prison and the two were both paroled in 1972 and they went right back to work for Carmine Fatico at the Bergin Hunt and Fish Club with the rest of their old friends. Gotti was placed in the illegal gambling racket and quickly proved himself to be an extremely effective enforcer. Fatico was arrested on loansharking charges that same year which meant he could no longer associate with people who were known felons.

At this time, the list of made men had not been added to since before 1960 so Gotti was not technically an official member of the mafia. A made man is an official member of the family. They are sworn in via a secret ceremony where they promise loyalty to the Family above everything else, even their lives. This ceremony is sometimes referred to as getting straightened out or getting your button. Made men are often referred to as Friends of Ours, Nice Fellows or Good Fellows. Even before the freeze, it was common for hopeful made men to spend years as associates, waiting for the day they are deemed to be reliable enough money earners to be found worthy. A made man will always have Italian blood.

Additionally, made men are forced to take a separate vow that says they will never cooperate with the authorities, a vow that is no longer taken as seriously as those at the top would like, though when Gotti ultimately took the oath it was deadly serious. Even still, it is enough to make a member of the Family who is willing to talk to police a prized commodity.

Promotions were thus rarely given out to those who had not reached this rank. Nevertheless, Fatico left him as acting capo of the crew in his place. With this promotion he regularly reported to Dellacroce at the Ravenite social club and reconnected with his mentor as well. The pair were a natural match for one another, both gambled heavily, enjoyed profanity and were known to be extremely violent. Dellacroce had liked Gotti when he was younger, but now he soon took the young man more formally under his wing.

In 1973, the nephew of Emanuel Gambino was murdered after being kidnapped and Ruggiero and Gotti were both assigned to the hit team assigned to bring down the man responsible, rival gangster James McBratney. The initial capture of McBratney is botched and the squad eventually catches up with him at a local bar where he is shot dead. Gotti is seen by several eyewitnesses and is arrested for the murder in June of 1974. Despite the evidence against him, he manages to get a plea deal for just four years on an attempted manslaughter charge as he was not the one to actually execute the hit.

Chapter 2
MADE MAN

When Gotti is released from prison in July 1977, after serving just half of his sentence, he is soon initiated into the Gambino family now firmly under the command of Paul Castellano. Gotti is formally made the capo of the Bergin crew to replace Fatico. He and his crew now reported directly to Dellacroce as part of a concession made to keep Dellacroce on after the transfer of power.

This concession was made to Dellacroce as Castellano had come into power via a convoluted play that saw him jumping several ranks out of order, something that Dellacroce could have easily taken violent issue with if he had not be properly sated. To ensure this was not the case, Castellano gave Dellacroce essentially unlimited control over the capos under his command. While this situation worked to cement his power, it eventually created two competing families under the same banner, those who were loyal to Castellano in heart and mind, and those that were loyal to Dellacroce in reality and Castellano only in name.

While they overlapped from time to time, the two factions develop distinct personalities, largely based around the activities they had control of. The Castellano wing tended to be more white-collar as they ran things like bid-rigging and racketeering for the garment, meat, cartage and construction industries. The Dellacroce faction, on the other hand, was much more blue collar and tended to stick to hijacking, gambling and loan-sharking. While the two groups didn't exactly get along, they at least kept the peace with one another until Dellacroce eventually died in 1985.

With Gotti at its head, the Bergin crew flourishes and quickly become the biggest earners for Dellacroce who takes Gotti on as his protégé. Besides getting a piece of the action from the Bergin crew's dealing, Gotti also started a loan sharking business while also receiving a paycheck from a job at a plumbing supply business that he didn't need to actually show up for. The FBI also has reason to believe that he was financing drug deals at this time though this was never confirmed as all such dealings were, at the time, kept strictly off the books.

Part of Gotti's territory included a substantial gambling network, which was akin to giving a drunk control of a distillery. Gotti was known to be a prodigious gambler all of his life, with losses of as much as $50,000 coming up regularly on a weekend of betting at the races. At one point he won an alleged $225,000 from the Brooklyn Number, a sort of local lottery run by the Gambinos, and then lost it all after a pair of unlucky nights shooting craps the very next week.

Despite his ever-deepening ties to the criminal underworld, Gotti tried to keep his young family separate from business. This did not include his oldest son John "John Jr" Angelo Gotti who was a known associate of the mob by 1982.

In December of 1978 Gotti helped pull off one of the biggest unrecovered cash robberies in history. The Lufthansa Heist took place at the Kennedy Airport and Gotti arranged for the getaway vehicle to end up as scrap metal at a friendly Brooklyn scrap yard. The driver failed to do as he was told, however, and parked the van near his girlfriend's house instead. The van was quickly recovered and numerous valuable fingerprints were taken from it.

In March of 1980, Gotti's youngest son Frank was killed while riding a minibike by a man named John Favara. The death was ruled an accident, but Favara soon started receiving death threats and was then attacked by Victoria Gotti who hit him in the torso and face with a baseball bat several times when he came to apologize for what had happened. A few months later he was abducted and never seen again. While the Gottis were in Florida at the time, it is generally assumed that at least one of the Gotti's was involved in ordering the abduction to take place.

Gotti was indicted twice more before he moved on from being the capo for the Begin Crew, though both didn't come to fruition until he ascended to boss of the family. In 1984 he got into a fight with a refrigerator mechanic in September and was ultimately charged with assault as well as robbery. Gotti had slapped the man while one of Gotti's men took a little over $300 out of his pocket. The confrontation came about because Gotti's car was double parked in a spot in Queens. The money was taken out of spite, but the police report made it sound like a robbery. This wasn't necessarily any worse legally, but he thought the theft below him and the case continued to rankle him while it ran its course.

The next year he and Dellacroce, along with several other crew members, were all indicted for a large racketeering case by Assistant US Attorney Diane Giacalone. This indictment also showed Gotti that Willie Boy Johnson was working as a federal informant.

Chapter 3
TAKING THE THRONE

Gotti's plan to remove Paul Castellano didn't form all at once but rather grew to fruition over time as everything the other man did made Gotti feel as though he was too greedy and isolated to run the family effectively. What's more, like much of the family, he also disliked the man on a personal level as he felt Castellano lacked the street credibility that one could only acquire by coming up through the ranks with street level jobs the way that he and his friends had.

Furthermore, there was also an economic motive to Gotti's eventual takeover as he and Castellano had a longstanding disagreement over the split of the take that Gotti received from regular airport hijackings that were carried out under his supervision. In addition to this, Gotti was suspected to be getting more heavily into the drug trade at this time, something that Castellano was vehemently against, as history would prove multiple times before Gotti's story was through.

In August of 1983, Gene Gotti and Ruggiero are arrested for selling heroin based on recordings from a bug that was placed in Ruggiero's home. When Castellano found out, he demanded the tapes to see if Gotti was complacent in the deals but Ruggiero refused knowing they would certainly implicate Gotti. Castellano flew into a rage at the refusal and threatened to demote Gotti though nothing ever came from the threat and the tapes were never produced.

By this time Gotti has developed a reputation for being ruthless which he cultivated at every opportunity possible. He spoke to everyone, friends and enemies alike, in a way that could be best described as ferocious. This image was not formed by words alone, however, as he was willing to back up his boisterous talk with a fist or a gun if such were required. By this point he was already on record with the FBI dozens of times talking about how he enjoyed batting practice and cracking the heads of people who displeased him.

Gotti, who had started from nothing, had also developed an ego as large as his temper. He was known to become giddy at times when discussing how far he had come and how far he could yet still rise. He was still listed as being employed by a plumbing company but the only thing the FBI agents assigned to follow him ever saw him do was take meetings that appeared to be designed to help him foster the relationships he would need in the Family to get ahead in the long run.

The next year Castellano was indicted in a murder case committed by a Gambino hitman crew led by Roy Demeo. In 1985 he was indicted again, this time for the role he played in the American Mafia Commission. While Castellano was dealing with a seemingly never-ending parade of court appearances, Gotti was conspiring with other Gambino capos who were unhappy with the current leadership. This included Joseph "Joe Piney" Amone and Frank DeCicco, along with Robert DiBernado and Sammy Gravano who were soldiers. Gotti dubbed the group The Fist and claimed that if he didn't take Castellano out then Castellano would do the same to him first despite there being no evidence that this was the case or that Castellano had any reason to disrupt a status quo that was already working quite comfortably in his favor.

Armone's support was critical in this instance as he as an old-timer that was well-respected in the Mafia and had been in the Gambino family, as it was now called, since it was founded decades prior. His consent would lend the conspiracy the legitimacy that was needed for it to succeed, not just in killing Castellano, but in putting Gotti into his place.

This was due to the fact that it was a hard and fast rule in the mafia that you didn't kill a boss unless a majority of the Commission agreed to it. In fact, Castellano's eventual death marked the first such occurrence of Family on Family violence in nearly 30 years. Gotti understood the risks of the undertaking and knew that there would be too much at risk to bring any of the other bosses in on what he was going to do. Instead, he gained the support of key figures from his own generation among the Bonanno, Colombo and Lucchese families. He left out the Genoveses as Castellano was very close with Genovese boss Vincent "Chin" Gigante and letting him in on the plan would have been a huge tipoff. As such, Gotti could claim unofficial support from a majority of the families without Commission support. He also knew he could count on the consigliere of the Gambino family, Joseph Gallo, to back his play.

Soon, with the scent of change on the wind, many of Castellano's captains rallied around Gotti for one reason or another, one of which was Ralph Mosca, the copa of crew in Queens. He was known to be generally fond of Gotti, and also not fond of making waves so Gotti saw no reason not to trust him when he was assured that the crew in Queens would toe the line. One member of the crew was Dominick Lofaro who was at the same time also working for the New York State Organized Crime Taskforce. He was also a perfect example of why the Family had long been against selling drugs.

This policy had nothing to do with the sort of unconscionable things that go along with the drug trade, nor with the negative effect it can have on the neighborhoods that the Family called home. Rather, it was a purely self-interested policy that Gotti blithely tossed by the wayside in exchange for short-term profits. The reason for its existence was that New York

City treated drug dealing just as severely as it did murder and drug dealing was much more difficult to cover up, especially as those being murdered weren't civilians if it could at all be avoided.

For the Family, what this meant is that anyone arrested on drug charges would be facing a lengthy sentence that would be difficult to beat in most cases, making any plea deal the prosecution may want to hand out look extremely appetizing, particularly those who were lower on the totem pole and thus much more likely to be pinched when the heat came down. As a serious charge was considered anything more than four ounces of heroin or cocaine, getting into the drug trade would expose them to a significant amount of additional risk when compared to their more reliable, and subtle, ways of making money, each of which kept them comfortably cloaked in the shadows.

This didn't mean that no one ever dealt drugs under the previous regime, however, rather they did it in small amounts, on the side as the lure of the easy money of drugs was frequently too strong to ignore as was the promise of an income stream not directly taxed by the family. This was known as going off the record and it was generally understood that anyone caught doing it was going to be dealt with via the strictest of penalties and often death. Dominic Lofaro had been caught, not by the Family, but by the police and, after being threatened with a life sentence for selling heroin, agreed to turn states evidence. Lofaro was a prized contact for the FBI as at this point only a handful of made men had ever broken their vows though if they had known how much that was going to change in the coming years they might have changed their minds.

Lofaro was given a personal taping device, which anyone can wear at any time in New York if they wish to tape their own conversations. He wore the device for nearly a year before he came into contact with John Gotti, but once he did, got him on tape confessing to taking part in an illegal gambling operation. This was enough to get the Task Force the court order they needed to plant an audio bug in Gotti's Bergin Hunt and Fish Club in March of 1985.

Throughout the rest of the year, this audio recorder, along with a subsequent phone tap would provide a detailed view into Gotti's life, though nothing that could be directly used in his impending racketeering case because they were recorded after he had been indicted. Unfortunately for the taskforce, their ability to eavesdrop on his communications ended in October of 1985, a few months before things got really interesting. They were not reinstalled until December 27 of that year.

Dellacroce died from cancer in December of 1985. Instead of allowing Gotti to succeed him as planned, Castellano changed the chain of succession and Bilotti was appointed to underboss with Thomas Gambino serving as acting boss. The new plan would have cut Gotti and his people out of the loop completely. This fact, coupled by the fact that Castellano missed Dellacroce's wake, felt like a huge slap in the face to Gotti and pushed him over the edge, ultimately causing him to move the timetable for his ascension plan forward.

While from Gotti's perspective Castellano made a conscious choice to avoid the funeral as a way of showing how he felt about Dellacroce, in reality the reason for his absence was much more benign. At this point Castellano was the defendant in a pair of federal racketeering cases, and the trial in which he also stood accused of murder was well underway. The funeral had simply slipped his mind, a dangerous lapse in judgement from a man who was already having trouble within his family, though he didn't know it yet.

December 16, 1985 started off as a good day for Castellano, his trial was on recess for the day and he was just a few days away from a judge approved vacation in Florida. Days away from the courtroom in New York City were few and far between so he had a full schedule of meetings with various captains planned. The day would end with a 5 pm meeting with a number of his captains at Sparks Steakhouse in Manhattan, in one of the busiest areas of the busiest cities in the entire world. This was the time Gotti chose to strike and when the boss and the underboss arrived they were ambushed and gunned down by roughly a dozen men who had been waiting for them in cars and on benches surrounding the restaurant as they had ended up getting stuck in traffic. Gotti watched the hit take place from a nearby car.

Castellano and his underboss weren't carrying any weapons, after all they were going to a friendly sit down at a crowded restaurant in midtown where there would be no chance for any action as there would be too many civilians which would make a hit too risky. At 5:26 pm, Castellano's car stopped in front of Sparks restaurant. Two of the men approached the car, one went for Castellano, the other for the underboss while the other men, and Gotti, watched on. Each of the men were shot six time in the head and the upper chest and a witnessed later recalled that someone made sure to double tap Castellano before fleeing the scene.

A few days after the murder, Gotti was named as part of a three-man committee to run the Gambino family until a new boss could be elected. The other two members of the committee were DeCicco and Gallo. An internal investigation into the murder was also scheduled though practically everyone knew where the hit had originated from. Despite this fact, Gotti was formally named as the new boss of the family in January of 1986. DeCicco became the new underboss and Gallo became his consigliere.

While not officially named to the position until January, Gotti took on a new position in the minds of Americans almost immediately. Word on the street had him pinned as the future head of the family almost as soon as the murder occurred and everyone from police familiar with the Family to local newspaper vendors were suddenly talking about the man of the hour. Several reporters tried to talk to him around the time of Castellano's assassination but each time he declined. He likewise declined, through his attorney, to a voluntary interview the FBI had set up to discuss the incident.

While well on his way to securing his power, Gotti's plan wasn't perfect. First, he insulted half of his future family by not attending Castellano's wake, as further payback for the fact that Castellano had himself missed Dellacroce's wake a few weeks earlier. This mistake was then compounded by his appointment of Bilotti to underboss the following year instead of someone from the Castellano side of the family.

Despite being a murder suspect, Gotti didn't shy away from the police and FBI agents who regularly followed him when he was out on the town. He always road in a chauffeured car, not because he could afford to do so but because his driving record was as dirty as his criminal record. At this time there were whispers of him in the legitimate world, but few people yet new him by sight.

The detectives and agents who were currently following Gotti were understandably on edge, they were currently following a man wanted for a double murder while also keeping an eye out for indications that the most powerful family in one of the most powerful criminal enterprises in the world may be going to war. They knew that the murder of a boss need to be sanctioned and wondered if this one had been and, if not, what it would mean for the underworld as a whole.

At this time, Gotti and many of his captains held offices in the Ravenite Social Club. A social club is a common occurrence in New York City neighborhoods and is a place where friends can get together to play games and get out of the house. The family used it for other purposes, however and those following Gotti would regularly watch him visit the Ravenite, a fact that would ultimately lead to his downfall.

While publicly he was full of bravado regarding his future, stakeouts at the time reveal that he was anything but certain of his future position. The parts of the family that were loyal to him held several meetings and it was unclear to those following if they were readying for war. On Christmas Eve, a pair of high dollar cars pulled up outside of the Ravenite Social Club and two men walked passed all the men who were obviously working security to go and see Gotti directly, the two men them embraced Gotti and kissed both his cheeks. He was in.

Chapter 4
BIG BOSS

Gotti quickly rose to fame in his new position. By 1986, the Gambino family was the most powerful mafia family in America, bringing in more than $500 million each year. Around this time, it is estimated that Gotti himself was making at least $5 million per year, though that number could be as high as $15 million. In order to protect himself and his organization he forbid any of his people from taking any plea agreement that acknowledged the existence of the mafia to the FBI under penalty of death.

Of note around this time is that in January of that year Vincent Gotti, Gotti's brother, was sentenced to six years in jail for the sale of cocaine. Vincent wasn't working for the Family at the time of his arrest and not a single member of the Family attended his sentencing. Meanwhile brother Gene, currently awaiting movement on his heroin case, stood by his brother, unaware that much of what was being said was being heard by unfriendly ears.

On January 13, 1986, Gotti appeared publicly for the first time since the murders. He attended a pretrial hearing for his racketeering case at the US District Court House in Brooklyn. The press showed up in full force to get a look at the new boss and pepper him with questions. When asked if he was the new boss of the Gambino Family, Gotti replied, "I'm the boss of my family, my wife and kids at home." While this wasn't much, it was more than the press was used to getting out of a Family man, and Gotti looked the part to boot. He was well-groomed and stylish with his soon to be customary double-breasted suit and camel hair overcoat. He acted more like a politician who was too dignified to respond to slanderous questions from his opponent as opposed to a criminal hiding from the light of day.

After a brief period of time, Gotti left the courthouse and climbed back into his lawyer's black Cadillac and drove away, leaving a positive impression among reporters in his wake, especially considering that he was facing three separate murder charges against eight separate defendants.

During this time Gotti maintained a genial public facing image as he tried to downplay news reports of his more gruesome exploits. He was known to regularly offer coffee to the FBI agents assigned to follow him and regularly waved and asked them about their families.

Gotti was officially named boss of the Gambino family on January 16, 1986 at the practically unheard-of age of 45. Frank DeCicco was made underboss as planned and Joe N. Gallo retained his position as consigliere. Mosca attended the event which meant that Lofaro, and thus the FBI, new about it later that night. DeCicco was also given a no-show job with the International Brotherhood of Teamsters along with a crew to call his very own. In fact, the crew he inherited was the one previously run by Thomas Bilotti. At the same time, Angelo Ruggiero took over Gotti's former Hunt and Fish crew which included Richard, Peter and Gene Gotti. Each of the other Gotti's had minor criminal records, except for Gene who, in addition to his heroin case was also already a defendant in a racketeering case in Brooklyn.

While initially tense, after that first meeting at the Ravenite Club, Gotti's assentation was all but assured, this meeting just made it official. Now it didn't matter that he was already under indictment or that he could be sent away for life at any time, all that mattered to Gotti was that he had put all of his cards on the table and come out on top. He went out and bought himself a

Mercedes-Benz SEL for $60,000 cash to celebrate.

The first day on the job he learned that Castellano had regularly been taking money from the widow of a former captain who only had a small amount of money coming in each year, a practice that he promptly discontinued. He also reworked a few moneymaking schemes so that the soldiers would receive a larger piece of the pie and called off a strike under the assurance that the concrete plant, that was to be the target, sweetened the pie a little bit.

On January 23, the new Gambino trifecta of Gotti, DeCicco and Gallo headed to the Helmsley Palace Hotel in Manhattan to meet with record executives who were looking to gather capital for the release of a new artist. The introductions were made by Armone. As such, the news made it to the authorities and both police and newspaper reporters were on hand when the trio stepped off the elevator after the meeting. While all three men declined to be interviewed in the press, video of Gotti, looking well dressed and slightly sinister was broadcast coast to coast with a story about the potential investment.

Gotti had more to attend to than making national headlines and helping old ladies, however, he also had to punish his subordinates who got out of line. There were a few captains who had not come around as easily as Armone, and one of these was Anthony Gaggi. Gotti learned of this fact when he received a call from a loyal solider informing him of a dispute regarding a restaurant in Brooklyn. Family members had been brought in and the landlord need to know that they were on the level. The solider said that Gaggi wanted Gotti to come down and see him but Gotti insisted that it go the other way. In the meantime, he said, everything else would be on hold until after the sit down. Three days later Angelo was heard complaining that he had to visit someone about the restaurant problem and then two days after that the restaurant burned down.

Conversations of Gotti's that were overheard during this period of time show that while he was occasionally uncertain about some aspects of his position, he was very certain of himself in the role in general. At one point he was heard to say, "I don't know about concrete, steel or construction but I got a lot of spies in the streets so I know everything."

No all of the new business was in high stakes areas, Gotti quickly proved that he was willing to go wherever there was a dollar to be made. One such instance of this was an ice cream shop the Family had acquired some years before. Unfortunately for Gotti the business wasn't booming. He apparently loved ice cream but the numbers didn't add up. He also didn't like that, despite the fact that he owned a portion of the shop, he couldn't visit and get free ice cream because surveillance in the area was too hot. His anxiousness was understandable, after all he was dealing with much larger stakes commerce these days.

At the same time, he was fielding propositions for new business from far and wide including casinos in Puerto Rico and a gasoline scam that was estimated to be worth more than a million dollars in the Midwest. Gotti was able to freely receive the visitors who brought these propositions, as he had recently been given bail regarding the indictment of his federal case. Along with finding time for all the people bearing gifts and business deals, Gotti also had to find time for his lawyers as in order to ensure he kept his new status, he would need to stay out of jail.

It was also around this time that Gotti gained another nickname, the Teflon Don. This started with the man Gotti had previously assaulted in the park, Romual Piecyk, who was, at the time, planning to testify against Gotti for slapping him and taking his money. While the case was waiting to go trial, FBI agents were also meeting with a pair of informers who were inside the Gambino family. While they would never take the stand, their tips enable countless busts between 1966 and 1990. These sources were contacted after every major event in Gotti's life, such as his run-in with Piecyk.

In fact, Piecyk, whose grand jury testimony was what set the entire trial in motion in the first place, only moved forward with the whole thing because he didn't know who Gotti was. Officials later claim that he was told that they were connected, but Piecyk claimed he only ever knew they were "punks". However, with Gotti's new level of fame, he was suddenly learning everything he hadn't previously known. That, and the boss's new connections were enough to make sing a different tune. He did in fact still appear in court, though willingly only for the opening arguments and then only to support Gotti. He summed up his plan to a reporter before entering the courthouse. "I'm not going to go against Mr. Gotti, I'm going in on his behalf. I don't want to hurt Mr. Gotti."

In addition to now having his victim in his corner, Gotti also had ace Family lawyer Bruce Cutler who was especially adept at getting a certain type of people out of especially sticky situations. Prior to 1981 he had been one of the best prosecutors in the state but the money on the other side of the fence had been too alluring and he now used the skills that the state used to prize so highly to get people like Gotti out of the courtroom and back onto the street as quickly as possible.

During the trial, Cutler painted Piecyk as a drunken bully who had picked a fight with Colletta while he was in the restaurant with Gotti. He then claimed that Gotti intervened in the scuffle to pull the little man off the much bigger man. The story ended with Piecyk stumbling off and dropping his money in the scuffle. Piecyk, who was due to testify the next day, failed to appear, having instead checked himself into the hospital for elective surgery on his shoulder. When he ultimately did appear in court he could not identify the man who had assaulted him in the courtroom that day.

The prosecutor tried to come at the question from numerous different angles but Piecyk was resolute. He could not remember what the men in the incident looked like, their general outlines or even the way they had been dressed. The newspapers summed up the event with the headline "I Forgotti". Authorities were later alerted to the fact that Gambino family members had cut Piecyk's brake lines, stalked him and made threatening calls to his home prior to the trial. He decided to stand down over fear for his life and that of his pregnant wife.

The following morning the judged denied a motion to use the grand jury testimony for evidence rather than the in-person testimony.

The judge replied that while the memory of the witness was certainly dead or missing, they were still very much alive so the testimony would stand. With nothing left to say in the matter, Gotti left the courtroom soon after, not necessarily a free man but one certainly freer than he was when he entered.

In March of 1986 Gotti, ever afraid to fly, traveled by limo to Florida in order to get some sun prior to the jury selection of his racketeering trial. On the day he left, one of his codefendants in the case, Armond Dellacroce, the son of Gotti's mentor, disappeared. He had already plead guilty to his own racketeering charge after his father had died the previous year and was currently waiting on sentencing and expecting at least 20 years in prison. Authorities also felt that he was well on his way to being willing to make a deal. It was assumed that his flight risk was low and he had been regularly checking in with pretrial services as he promised he would.

Diane F. Giacalone, an assistant US attorney, was overseeing the case after first leading the three-year investigation that lead to the arrest in the first place. The process was long and tiresome but Giacolone was tireless and continued to dog Gotti for the rest of his time as a free man. Dellacroce was a victory sure, at least until his disappearance, but he was just the appetizer, Gotti would be the main course.

Jury selection for the racketeering case started in April of of 1986. Willie Boy Johnson and Gene Gotti and Carneglia all stood trial along with Gotti. Even though he had been outed as an informant, Willie Boy still declined to turn state's evidence for the case. The Gambinos managed to compromise the case by getting George Pape onto the case as a juror despite the fact that he was secretly friends with Bosko Radonjich, the boss of the Westies. Pape then agreed to sell his vote on the jury for $60,000.

In the case, Gotti and the other were accused of having knowingly violated federal law which stated it was illegal to commit individual crimes as part of a large illegal enterprise, in this case the Gambino Family. Carneglia stood accused of killing Albert Gelb an officer of the court in Brooklyn who was shot before he could testify against Carneglia's brother who was facing a gun possession charge. Carneglia's brother John was also indicted in the case but he too, had vanished.

On the second day of the trial, Giacalone caused a scene by claiming that twice in the past week multiple potential witnesses had been approached by unidentified men who asked them about specifics relevant to the case. Giacalone promised that if anything similar happened again, she would work to revoke the bail of each of the defendants. Two days later, Cutler complained to the judge of the carnival atmosphere that Giacalone's statements had created and asked for a gag order that he was hoping would be denied, which it was.

When the jury selection began again, several of the potential jurors told the selecting attorney that they were having a hard time keeping an open mind. By the end of the first week, the jury selection process was already taking far longer than anticipated and the two-month timeframe for the entire trial was already getting ready to go off the rails. Things were proceeding in just the way that Cutler had hoped, if they kept up in this fashion then he would be able to get an extension on the trial, or possibly a mistrial if things could be ultimately strung along until the trial itself had started. A rival Family, however, had other plans that altered the course of the trial, and perhaps the rest of Gotti's life.

On April 13, 1986, DiCicco was killed with a car bomb after he visited the home of James Failla, a Castellano loyalist. The bombing was handled by members of the Lucchese family under order from the boss of the Lucchese family, Anthony Corallo as a means of avenging his fallen comrade. Gotti was supposed to go with DiCicco but canceled at the last moment. The bomb went off anyway when the man DiCicco brought with him was mistaken for Gotti. This was a low blow by Corallo as the American Mafia had long had a firm rule against bombs due to their potential to harm innocent civilians. As such, the Gambino's initially suspected the Zips, a branch of the Sicilian mafiosi, to be behind the bombing.

After the bombing, the judge presiding over the case rescheduled to avoid a jury corrupted by the publicity. At the same time, Giacalone revoked Gotti's bail in an effort to prevent witness tampering. Regardless, from behind bars Gotti still ordered the murder of Robert DiBernardo which was carried out by Sammy Gravano. Ruggiero and DiBernado had both been trying to succeed DeCicco and Ruggiero accused DiBernardo of challenging Gotti for head of the family. As Ruggiero was also under indictment, he instead promoted Joseph Armone to the position of underboss.

In the opening statement of the trial in September of that year, Bruce Cutler, Gotti's defense attorney tried to spin it so the jury would believe the entire existence of the Gambino crime family was a malicious perpetration by the FBI against Gotti and the legitimate business men that he worked with. The primary defense strategy was to attack the credibility of each of the prosecution's witnesses by discussing the crimes they had committed prior to turning state's evidence.

In addition, Cutler called as a witness Matthew Traynor a potential witness for the prosecution who was dropped at the last minute. Traynor testified that Defense Attorney Giacalone offered him not only drugs in exchange for his testimony but also her underwear to use for sexual purposes as well. These accusations were dismissed by the judge after the trial and Traynor was ultimately charged with perjury.

Nevertheless, despite Traynor's actions, and a subpar case by the prosecution, a majority of the jurors were initially in favor of convicting Gotti of his crimes. With Pape on the inside, the worst that Gotti could expect was a hung jury. Pape did better than that, however, and was able hang in for the long-term while also spreading rumors that made the other jurors fear for their own safety should deliberations continue indefinitely. Ultimately, they came back with a verdict of not guilty on all charges in March of 1987. Eventually, Pape would be convicted of obstruction of justice for his part in the conviction and sentenced to three years in prison.

As the country was just coming off the extreme success of the Mafia Commission Trial at this point, the fact that Gotti was acquitted was seen as a serious upset to the status quo. This only increased his public person and his fame continued to grow to nearly legendary status. This is when he gained the name "Teflon Don" because charges apparently would not, could not, stick to him.

While Gotti managed to escape conviction, his peers were not so lucky. Aremone and Gallo had also both been hit with racketeering charges in 1986 and were then both convicted in December 1987. Likewise, the heroin trial for Gene Gotti and Ruggiero commenced in June of 1987.

Prior to these convictions, Gotti let Gallo retire and promoted Sammy Gravano in his place while setting up Frank Locascio to serve as underboss for when Aremone went to prison. The Gambinos managed to successfully tamper with the jury for the heroin trial, which lead to a mistrial. Ruggiero was terminally ill by this point and was released in 1989. Gotti never contracted him as he blamed Ruggiero for the misfortunes the family was now facing.

Starting in January of 1988, and against the advice of Gravano, Gotti started having all of his capos meet him at the Ravenite Social Club every week at the same time. This decision made it much easier for the FBI surveillance team to identify and record the hierarchy of the family in a way that had previously been impossible. It also gave the FBI strong circumstantial evidence that Gotti was the boss based on the assumption that the meetings were a public display of loyalty. The FBI was then also able to bug the Ravenite, though nothing ever came of the recordings taken from the initial set of bugs.

1988 was also notable in that it saw the first meeting of the Commission since the trial. At the end of 1987, the FBI had warned Gotti that they had recorded the consigliere of the Genovese family discussing planning a hit on the Gotti brothers. The meeting in 1988 was an attempt to avoid an all-out war as the heads of the families met to tell one another that they had no knowledge of the violence that was being perpetrated on each other and to indicate that they were going to be more willing to communicate with each other moving forward.

The meeting also served as the time to invite Victor Orena to join the Commission. Gotti also put up for admission Joseph Massino and Bonannos, but Gigante, unwilling to give Gotti a guarnateed majority with council matters blocked them.

Despite this fact, Gotti was still able to take control of the DeCavalcante crime family, based in New Jersey before the end of the year. According to an informant who spent years as a DeCavalcante capo, on the day of the wake for the former leader of the family, Gotti showed up in force and demanded that the new boss John Riggi agree to run the family as an affiliate of the Gambinos. This arrangement lasted until Gotti's death.

1988 also marked another important moment in Gotti's life, Christmas Eve was the day his son was officially initiated into the Gambino family. Gravano officially held the ceremony to fend off accusations of nepotism but, nevertheless, John Jr. was immediately promoted to capo.

1989 started off with a bang for Gotti as on January 23 he was arrested while leaving the Ravenite based on charges that he had order a hit on John O'Connor a local union official in 1986. Connor's is believed to have first ordered an attack on a restaurant that was associated with the Gambino's that had not paid the fees it owed to the union. O'Connor was then shot and wounded by one of the Westies who botched the job. The FBI's case was based on the testimony of failed Westies hitman James McElroy as well as a taped conversation of Gotti stating that he intended to "bust up" O'Connor.

With the best lawyers money can buy, Gotti was quickly released from jail on a $100,000 bond. Proving himself the Teflon Don once more, he is acquitted on all charges. However, it was later discovered that an FBI bug had picked up Gotti discussing how his men had fixed the jury the same way as they had during the racketeering case. The FBI knew about the information at the time, they just chose to withhold the information because they knew it would lead to Gotti assuming he was being bugged.

Chapter 5
FINAL BUST

The final case against Gotti began being constructed in 1989 when members of the Eastern District Strike Force and federal prosecutors in Manhattan started leaning more heavily on the people associated with Gotti and gave them a choice: speak truthfully before a grand jury or face a lengthy prison sentence. One by one, grand jury subpoenas started showing up on the doorsteps of soldiers in the Gambino family. Throughout this time, Gotti's rules on speaking to authorities were clear, be honest when at all possible, forget details when things get specific and lie when you had to.

Numerous different men were subpoenaed including Thomas Spinelli a soldier from

Brooklyn who was linked to the murders at Sparks based on the fact that his capo, Jimmy Failla was one of the men who was going to meet with Castellano on the evening. Nevertheless, it was enough to make him a potential grand jury witness, especially as he had already testified in an earlier case after he received a subpoena in the mail to do so. He then made the crucial mistake of promising not to expose himself to perjury by saying things that were obviously lies.

While he didn't know much about what happened at Sparks, he did know enough to link the Gambino family to the private sanitation racket which was of ongoing interest to a variety of different agencies. The threat of perjury left him guessing what the grand jury already new as prosecutors mercilessly peppered him with questions on all aspects of Family life. The other soldiers in Spinelli's crew passed along what he was doing to Gotti who immediately decided that he had to be taken care of. Gravano ultimately lured Spinelli to a factory in Brooklyn where he was shot to death.

Another particularly relevant witness was Tommy Gambino who had been set to take over after Paul Castellano prior to Gotti taking control of the family. Gambino understood where the winds were blowing, however, and quickly assured Gotti that he had no desire to take control of the family back. Gotti rewarded Gambino with a cushy crew from which he made millions without having to get his hands dirty at all. Being subpoenaed was a new experience for Gambino who had previously been largely anonymous as far as the authorities were concerned.

Overall, he was called before a grand jury four times and each time his efforts to be evasive became more and more extreme. By the end of his time being questioned he had ventured into the nonsensical, easily recalling events from decades before but being unable to recall simple, nonincriminating details from meetings he had recently had with Gotti and other Family members. His evasiveness was enough to warrant a perjury charge. His lawyers hoped to get him out of it by saying that he was being target based on his father and occasional associations with Gotti, but Gotti felt that the whole thing painted to negative a picture of him.

Around the same time, the FBI had also managed to crack underboss of the Philadelphia Family Philip Leonetti which was bad for Gotti for multiple reasons. The first of which is that Leonetti was the highest-ranking Family member to roll over so far, and the second was that Gotti had met with Leonetti when he took over the Gambinos and indicated vaguely that he was now running the show. He couldn't remember the specifics but knew that Leonetti might.

In truth, Gotti was starting to feel boxed in on all sides. The pending case against him could easily carry a life sentence and he now knew that multiple grand juries were being convened against him. He grew more and more fearful of being listened to by the FBI, taking to talking to his men while walking the streets as much as the weather prevented. He also felt safe to talk in two other places, the first of which was the hallway leading to the private apartments that were situated above the Ravenite, there was a rear landing on the hallway where he could stay without anyone outside being able to see him. He still spoke in whispers but spoke about clandestine matters that never would have been brought up in the club itself.

The second location was the home of Nettie Cirelli, the Family widow Gotti had previously helped. who lived above the Ravenite and severed as its caretaker for several decades. Whenever Gotti needed to make use of her home, he would give her a few dollars to go to the store. Netti's was used for only the most high-level conversations, and even then, only when the stereo was on full blast.

By the end of 1989, the task force was able to secure as many as nine informants inside the Gambino family which was more than they had been able to manage in any other mafia related sting up until that point. It showed just how disliked Gotti was and also how lax security about such things had become since he took over. One particularly interesting piece of information they were able to uncover is that after his grand jury hearing, Tommy Gambino had made a beeline for the Ravenite to have a meeting with Gotti at Nettie's place.

At this point Nettie's place went from a closely guarded secret to an openly known one among the roughly 50 men that used the club on a regular basis. With so much action in the area, the taskforce was able to secure permission to bug the place and planted an audio bug in her living room as well as one in the hallway that

Gotti was also now known to use as a safe space. Almost immediately Gotti was picked up discussing acts that would obstruct justice which would later be used in the racketeering case.

On December 11, 1990, a taskforce of local officers along with FBI agents raided the Ravenite Social Club, arresting Frank Locascio, Gravano and Gotti. While in the back of the police car Gotti was heard to bet Gravano that he would beat whatever the current charge was with three to one odds. The charges ended up being racketeering once more, including five counts of murder (Louis Dibono, Liborio Milito, Robert DiBernardo, Bilotti and Castellano, tax evasion, bribery, obstruction of justice, running an illegal gambling operation, loansharking and conspiracy to commit murder.

The hearing regarding bail and other pretrial matters was held on December 21, 1990. Prior to the start of the proceedings, the prosecution realized that they also had Gotti on tape confessing to knowing of the murder of DiBono, which they had previously missed. During the hearing they played a wide variety of excerpts from conversations Gotti had held in Nettie's, each discussing a different murder.

Unlike with his previous trials, Gotti was denied bail based on information found in the tapes that the FBI's had heard. Additionally, longtime lawyers Gerald Shargel and Bruce Cutler were not allowed to defend the men as the prosecution argued that they may be called as witnesses during the trial and were essentially a part of the evidence. The lawyers, the prosecution argued, not only were aware of the criminal activity that was going on but took things a step further and acted as in-house counsel for the Gambino organization specifically.

Nevertheless, the move was controversial, denying the men their basic right to choose their own lawyer could easily look as though Giacalone was looking for revenge after her previous loss. The prosecution mulled over the decision for a long time prior to making a decision, but the more they did so the more they felt that the evidence justified it. For the trial, Gotti hired Albert Krieger, an attorney from Miami who had previously successfully worked with Joseph Bonanno.

The tapes that the FBI had revealed would ultimately prove much more valuable than anyone realized at the time as they also captured Gotti speaking poorly of his newly appointed underboss Sammy Gravano. Gotti went on to call Gravano greedy and to say that he was the main instigating force behind the murders of Dibono, Milito and DiBernardo. Gotti eventually tried to reconcile but Gravano was not swayed. Gotti left and Gravano found himself doubting his future in the mob as well as his chance of beating a potential murder rap without Shargel to help him along. It was this fact that led him to decide to turn states evidence against Gotti, formally agreeing to testify in mid-November 1991.

He first reached out via a secret message that was sent to the FBI saying he would not remain loyal to someone who clearly tried to pin murders on him and also spoke negatively about him behind his back. As such, he was willing to make a deal, but only if life in prison was taken off the table. Negotiations for the deal took weeks of back and forth between the FBI who didn't want to appear to lenient to a man who had killed more than a dozen people, and Gravano confident that he held all the cards.

At the end it was all worth it for the FBI, however, as Sammy agreed to speak out against Gotti, becoming the first underboss in the history of the American Mafia to do so. He went on to identify, in great detail, the logistics of the 10-man hit squad that murdered Castellano and where all the major players, including Gotti, were placed. As an added bonus, he also admitted to fixing the 1987 trial. Some members of the prosecution wondered about using someone like Gravano as such a key witness to the case, but his unique viewpoint and clear perspective on all elements of the case made him too valuable not to use.

To further increase his value to the prosecution, Gravano also agreed to testify against anyone else that the government needed him to, regardless of who it was. He would gladly help to dismantle all of the mob if it meant that he would serve just five years in prison.

Gotti and Cocascio were both tried in District Court by Judge Leo Glasser. The trial began jury selection in January 1992, making use of an anonymous jury that would be fully sequestered during the trial to prevent the Gambino family from affecting the outcome. This was the first time a jury had ever been sequestered in the history of the Brooklyn Federal Court. Outside the courtroom during the early days, Gotti supporters continuously ran to the press with stories of Gotti buying presents for children in the hospital and of a time when Gotti urged some soldiers to return stolen religious relic.

During the jury selection process, Gotti was calm but this quickly faded as two big news stories started making the front page of the newspapers. The first was that Giacalone was declaring the previous trial had been fixed and the second outlined what Gravano was expected to testify about during the upcoming trial. These stories dashed the myth of the Teflon Don, just when they would have benefited Gotti the most. What's more, they negated the public opinion campaign that the defense was trying to create as well.

The trial proper got underway about a month later with the prosecutors starting out by playing tapes of Gotti discussing the family's business including several different murders that he approved of and his plan to eliminate Castellano. Next, they brought forth a witness in the Sparks hit who identified Gambino soldier John Carnelia as one of Bilotti's shooters. Gravano was brought out to testify on March 2. When he took the stand, he confessed to his place in the Gambino family and also described, in extreme detail the sum total of the conspiracy to murder Castellano, how it was executed and what the aftermath of the murder truly was.

He discussed, in brutal detail, the 19 murders that he had been a part of up until that point because murder was a way of life for the Family. He spoke for nearly nine days straight and it wasn't until that third day that he finally looked Gotti straight in the face and the two engaged in a fierce stare down. Sammy's face was a mask of indifference and Gotti wore a thin smile but anger burned brightly in both men's eyes. Neither man blink nor broke the stare until the prosecution asked its next question.

On the final day of his testimony, Gravano summed up the relationship he had with Gotti by saying, "He barked and I bit." The defense was unable to shake Gravano during cross-examination, likely because he was completely truthful, and he went down as the star witness from the trial. After further tapes and testimonies, the FBI rested its case on March 24. In their final argument, the prosecution reminded the jurors that what they had heard covered only six hours of recorded conversations between Gotti and others. Only six hours where they discussed murders and illegal activity across the spectrum. They were left pondering all the things they hadn't been privy too.

During most days of the trial it was common for a palpable sense of danger to fill the courtroom. Gotti's speech and mannerisms were filled with menace and the number of federal marshals stationed in the courtroom was doubled. The trial had to be put on hold three sperate times due to bomb threats and, privately, the judge for the case admitted that he had received numerous death threats and was under 24-hour protection.

To contrast the tense atmosphere, some days would prove to be as carefree and fun as a day at a carnival. This was caused by the steady parade of celebrities of all stripes that the Family was able to scrounge up to sing Gotti's praises. These included actors Anthony Quinn, Mickey Rourke, Al Lewis, John Amos, singer Jay Black, civil rights leader Roy Innis and boxer Renaldo Snipes.

This did not always go as planned, however, as several of the celebrities didn't play along as well as Gotti would have liked. For example, while Mickey Rourke was initially positive about the time he spent with Gotti, later on he refused to answer additional questions and quickly sped away from the courthouse. Anothony Quinn stuck to his role much more thoroughly, however, at one point even trying to go over and shake Gotti's hand, something that was forbidden by the federal marshals guarding Gotti at all times.

It would all prove to be for nothing, however, as five of the defense's six witnesses were eventually ruled to be either extraneous or irrelevant by the judge which only left Gotti's tax attorney, Murray Appleman, free to testify. In his testimony he admitted to working out a system whereby Gotti wouldn't have to pay taxes, allegedly without Gotti's prior knowledge. Additionally, things continued to go poorly for Gotti as his lawyer's motion for a mistrial was also denied. This led to Gotti becoming more and more hostile as the trial progressed, at one point calling Gravano a junkie and comparing the judge dismissing a juror to the tampering that occurred during the 1919 World Series. Things got so bad that the judge eventually threatened to have his removed from the courtroom.

The defense never even actively addressed any of the issues the prosecution brought up, except during cross examination, with the exception of the tax fraud charges. The tapes, coupled with Gravano's elaborate testimony gave them little to work with and less to do. Gotti's lawyer called the evidence suffocating in his final argument.

The trial ended on April 1, 1992 and it only took the jurors 14 hours to reach a verdict. They found Gotti guilty of all charges and Locasio guilty of all but one of his charges. At a press conference after the verdict was announced, Director of the New York Branch of the FBI James Fox was quoted as saying "The Teflon is gone, the Don is covered in Velcro and all the charges stuck." In June both defendants were sentenced to life in prison without the possibility of parole as well as a fine of $250,000 each.

On the day of the sentencing more than 1,000 people marched on the courthouse chanting and holding signs that read Free John Gotti. Several members of the crowd carried bullhorns and soon, urged on by John Jr.'s crew, they started rocking police cars and throwing rocks. With that, a full-blown riot had started and the Gotti supporters had the police outnumbered three to one. Inside, the guards barricaded the doors and stood by the windows, weapons drawn, but things quieted down before they had to use them.

At the same time, Gotti was already back at the federal holding pen in Manhattan where officials hurried to arrange his future sentence. Gotti was taken to serve his sentence at the US Penitentiary at Marion, Illinois. Most of his time was spent in relative solitary confinement and he was only allowed out of his cell for one hour each day. His final appeal on his sentence was rejected by the Supreme Court in 1994.

In July of 1996, Gotti was attacked by fellow inmate Walter Johnson who sucker punched him in the recreation room, leaving him battered and bleeding on the floor. This occurred because Gotti had used a racial slur to describe Johnson who had apparently overheard. In order to get revenge, Gotti sought out a pair of captains in the Aryan Brotherhood, Michael McElhiney and David Sahakian, and offered to pay them as much as an estimated $400,000 to kill Johnson. That next month, the word was put out to kill Johnson if the opportunity to do so arrived. Johnson was transferred to the Supermax prison in Colorado before an opportunity presented itself, however.

Despite outside pressure, Gotti refused to give up his title, something that he was technically allowed to keep until his retirement or death. Instead of finding a replacement, he had his son, John Jr., and his brother Peter relay his orders to the outside world. This continued until 1998, when by all accounts John Jr. was essentially running the family until he too was charged with racketeering.

Despite his father's orders to plead not guilty, John Jr. took a plea deal for six years and five months in prison. Publicly he has since cut all ties with the Gambino family. With John Jr. out of the picture, Peter Gotti assumed the role of acting boss and is believed to have officially taken on the boss title sometime shortly before his brother's death.

The indictment of John Jr. was the last straw for Victoria DiGiorgio Gotti who had, until this point, been able to maintain the façade of ignorance when it came to what her son did for work. She threatened to leave her husband if he didn't allow his son to leave the family behind.

In 1998, Gotti was diagnosed with throat cancer and transferred to the United States Medical Center for Federal Prisoners in Missouri for surgery. While the tumor was removed successfully, the cancer returned two years later and Gotti returned to the prison in Missouri where he lived out the rest of his days.

From 2000 onward, Gotti's condition advanced rapidly and he died June 10, 2002 at the age of 61. The Roman Catholic Diocese in Brooklyn forbade the family to hold a traditional Requiem Mass but allowed them to have a memorial mass after the body was buried.

The funeral took place in a nonchurch facility for approximately 300 onlookers who followed the procession, which wound past Bergin Hunt and Fish Club, to the graveyard. John Gotti's body was laid to rest in a crypt next to his son Frank. Frank Gotti's petition to attend his brother's funeral was denied. Despite Gotti's leadership and legacy, none of New York's crime families sent representatives to the funeral. In large part due to Gotti's tactics, more than half of all of the soldiers in the family were estimated to be in prison at this point and another third where expected or known to be informing for one agency or other. Gotti certainly left a legacy for the Family, though likely not the one he would have preferred.

Chapter 6
AFTER EFFECTS

While John Gotti was only freely controlling the Gambino family for less than a decade, the impact that his time in power had on the American Mafia as a whole cannot be overstated. To understand all he did, it is helpful to keep in mind the fact that between the time that Prohibition was declared and 1963, the country at large didn't publicly even acknowledge that the Mafia existed. Prior to the testimony of Joe Valachi, a Family soldier, J. Edgar Hoover, Director of the FBI, had actively been telling Attorney General RFK that the Mafia was just an unfounded rumor.

Prior to Gotti's reign, the mob was at the peak of its power, it controlled the Teamsters Union, along with its nearly endless pension fund and had also influenced the Democratic Party in numerous big cities. Furthermore, it dominated construction unions, private carting, owned Sonny Liston and dabbled in small time drug trades. At its prime it consisted of some 5,000 family members and roughly four or five times that in associates.

Today it is estimated to consist of no more than 500 family members. With increasing competition from the Colombians, Albanians, Chinese and Russians, the FBI now views the American Mafia, once their prime target, just the way they would any other gang competing for turf. After all, all of their legendary leaders are either dead or serving long prison sentences because of the way in which Gotti took the code of secrecy the Mafia had long lived by and blew the doors off the whole operation.

Right from the get-go, Gotti was a public figure, much more so than any other Family boss before him. He was constantly shown to love publicity which, in turn, brought on unneeded scrutiny to the organization at a time when the FBI was already taking an increasing interest in their actions. After all, his nickname was the Teflon Don, not Teflon John. This constant media attention was compounded by the fact that his activities were so predictable. Rather than having meetings and lunches with friends all over town where suspicions could be raised but nothing could be proven, Gotti made it clear to all who met him that he was the king. Making all of his capos come to him not only made it easier to track the comings and goings of the entire operation, it gave the FBI a clear location to focus on and a base of capos and soldiers to focus on turning into informants.

Furthermore, when Gotti killed Castellano, he also killed the primary force that was in charge of moving the Gambino Family, and thus much of the American Mafia as a whole, into modern times and more legitimate enterprises.

Castellano spent time trying to set up the types of deals that would take the Family out of the more illegal rackets and into something that would mean that no one would ever have had to fear the FBI again.

If Castellano was the future, Gotti took the Family back to the early days of the organization, he was never anything more than a hijacker and a street thug and his focus on expanding the business of the Family leaned in those directions. The assassination was carried out by other thugs like him, not even made men, and much of the reason it even took place in the first place was the distinction in the Family between the Castellano crew and the Dellacroce crew which was, at its heart, a class-based divide.

Throughout his time in power, Gotti had a history of disregarding those who had a more white-collar upbringing when compared with those who grew up on the streets like himself.

These men were often good at committing the types of crimes that Gotti was interested in fostering but were rarely good at the time of long-term thinking that had made many of his predecessors so successful. When they reached a point of real power, those in the know continuously shunned the spotlight.

Thomas Gambino was a good example of this, he lived his entire life in the Gambino family, more than 30 years at the time of the indictment before the grand jury, and had yet managed to remain a private figure for all of that time. He owned factories in the garment district and he was known, in the circles that new him at all, to be a movie producer. Contrast this to Gotti who was known to be the new head of the Gambino family around town, before he had even formally been offered the position.

The other bosses at the time were persona non-grata at all times. Chin Gigante never spoke on the telephone about anything important, ever;

Santos Trafficante never waved to fans outside his favorite social club, he had no fans and it would have been difficult for anyone outside his men to say just where his favorite social club was. Tony Slaerno wore suits of the same caliber as Gotti true, but he was certainly never photographed in them dancing at the local hotspot of the moment. Prior to 1967, local newspapers did not even have a picture of Gambio Sr. on file.

Falling in love with the spotlight has a history of ending poorly for Family members, starting with Joe Colombo who once closed down all the shops on Sullivan Street in order to allow all the employees to attend his civil rights rally in Columbus Circle. The other families quickly arranged to have him whacked as they felt his image brought too much heat to the other Families. Gotti's frenzy made everything that Colombo ever do seem tame by comparison. He first appeared on the cover of *Time Magazine* in 1986, and the cover essentially sealed his fate.

Once a made man starts talking about "his" public, only disaster will follow. This desire to be part of Manhattan's night life was what caused him to move the Gambino's base of operations out of Queens and to the Ravenite Social Club that six hours of footage would make so famous.

It is important to remember, that in most cases Family heads are approved by the group prior to any change of power taking place. If the Gambino family had continued to move through the traditional channels, Gotti never would have had a chance. Successful bosses had a certain penchant for following through on cost benefit analysis and doing anything that was needed to keep the Family a secret no matter what. Gotti simply lacked the people skills and the sophistication to manage the Mafia the way it needed to be managed. He was simply a cowboy killer and gambling addict whom the FBI heard ranting about his losses on the big game or the ponies far more than they ever did discussing ways in which the mafia could adapt to the changing times.

This attitude can also be seen in the fact that Gotti inducted his son into the Family as a Christmas present, making him the only boss to have family that was actively in the Family. The others all had families who used the influence and money their father made to further careers in legitimate business, but not Gotti, he was too busy basking in the name he had made for himself to truly stop and think what that name could ultimately cost him.

Finally, all the problems that Gotti brought to the mob were compounded by the fact that he reversed the long-standing stance the Family held on drugs. While some drug dealing always went on, the fact that it was off book, naturally kept sales to small person to person affairs that were difficult to pin down if the heat was on. Gotti's acceptance of the drug trade as a standard part of the operating procedure showed just how short-sighted he was, trading the security of the Family's long-term businesses for the high-risk high-reward promise of the drug trade.

The addition of the drug trade made it much easier for the authorities to create cases that could crack the historically silent Family members in a way that few other crimes they could be associated with could. While the charges were on par with murder, they were much easier to make stick because the suspects were always caught either with enough drugs to warrant an assumption of sales or through a sting where they were seen exchanging drugs for profits. There was nothing to hide behind and only cold hard facts standing between the soldiers and often 20 years or more in prison.

While Gotti's case was perhaps the highest profile, it was just the tip of the iceberg in the FBI's plans to dismantle American organized crime in a big way. While it will be impossible to ever get rid of the Mafia completely, there is too much history and potential mystique and intrigue for young Italian men with few prospects and a healthy disrespect for the law. However, with its main pillars a shadow of its former self the Mafia has once again taken to its traditional operations such as prostitution and gambling, most of which even takes place online these days, along with a new racket, credit card fraud.

The Mafia may survive, but thanks to John Gotti its glory days are most certainly behind it. Simply put, the code of silence that protected the Mafia for so many years has been broken, never to be put back together again. Gravano's high profile turn and subsequent fame means that every associate needs not just consider what it would be like to be a made man, they can just as easily imagine what it would be like to sell their story and become famous without having to deal with any of the politicking or murder that would come with a more traditional rise to the top in their line of work. What's more, he served as proof that a reckoning for breaking faith with the family isn't necessarily a sure and instantaneous thing, it is possible to live it up while thumbing your nose at the family as well. In an era where everyone is having these types of thoughts all of the time, it is impossible for anyone to trust anyone else.

This lack of trust means that when anyone one of them faces the prisoners' dilemma whereby two prisoners are both convicted of the same crime and told that if they say the other person did it they will walk free while the other person will receive a heavy sentence. Meanwhile, they are also told that if they say nothing and the other person also says nothing then they will both receive a light sentence. Prior to Gotti's rise, any two Family members would always choose to say nothing, knowing that their brothers would do the same. Now, however, with this no longer being the case, it suddenly always makes sense for everyone to always claim the other person did it because there is no guarantee they won't say the same.

Not only does this lack of trust make it easy for the FBI to do what it needs to do, it makes it impossible for the American Mafia to function cohesively and effectively in any way that would allow it to expand and reclaim its lost power. Until it slips back into the shadows completely, and forms a new set of oaths that its members can actually take seriously, it will remain a husk of its former self that is more active in popular culture than it is in the real world.

Conclusion

Thank you for making it through to the end of *Gotti: John Gotti American Mafia Boss*, let's hope it was informative and able to provide you with an insight into the life and times of John Gotti, perhaps the last truly powerful boss in the American Mafia. Gotti's rise to power was as meteoric as his ultimate fall from grace and while he may not have created the type of legacy that he was hoping for when he set out that cold December evening, his name will certainly be inscribed on the annals of American Mafia history for the harm his rule caused the organization as a whole.

Ever a popular figure in the pop culture of the time, Gotti has gone on to be the subject of countless movie and television shows, his influence and the idea of the American mafioso expanding far and wide, in much the way that his presence helped to bring down the code of silence that kept the American Mafia functioning for so many decades. When looked at from that perspective, he is perhaps the most valuable ally the FBI ever had when it comes to their war on organized crime.

Finally, if you found this book useful in anyway, a review on Amazon is always appreciated!

94889762R00054

Made in the USA
Columbia, SC
02 May 2018